This Book Belongs To

Color Testing Page

I WILL MAKE THE MOST OF TODAY

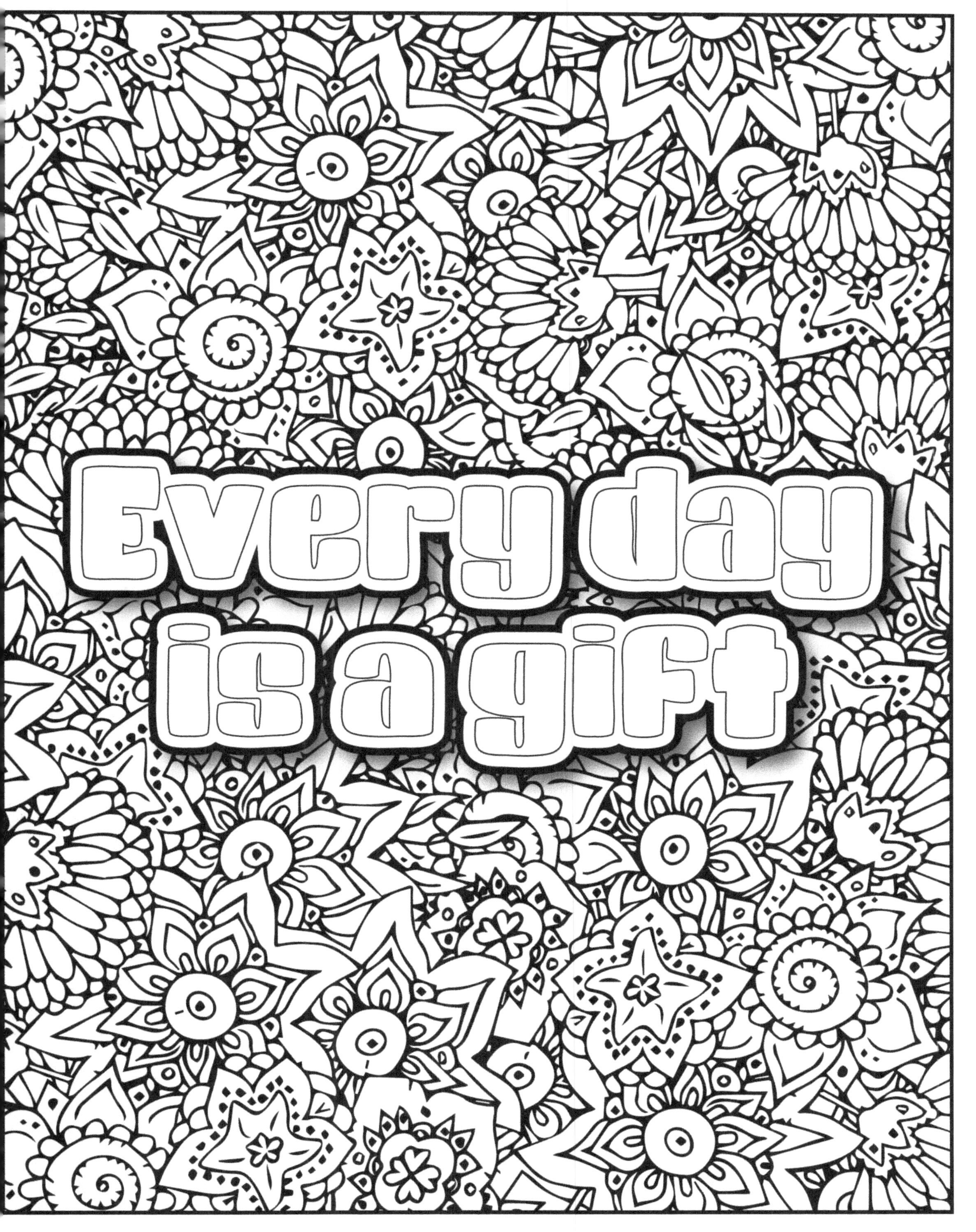

Every day
is a gift

THERE IS
NO WAY TO BE A
PERFECT MOTHER,
BUT A MILLION WAYS
TO BE A GOOD ONE

Life began
with waking up
and loving
my mother's face

Being a mother
is an attitude,
not a
biological relation

The best place
to cry is on
a mother's arms

All that
I am or ever
hope to be,
I owe to
my angel
mother

A mother's arms are more comforting than anyone else's

My mother
is
a walking
miracle

Being a mom
has made me
so tired.
And so happy

It's not easy
being a mother.
If it were easy,
fathers would
do it

Motherhood:
All love
begins and
ends there

The phrase
'working mother'
is redundant

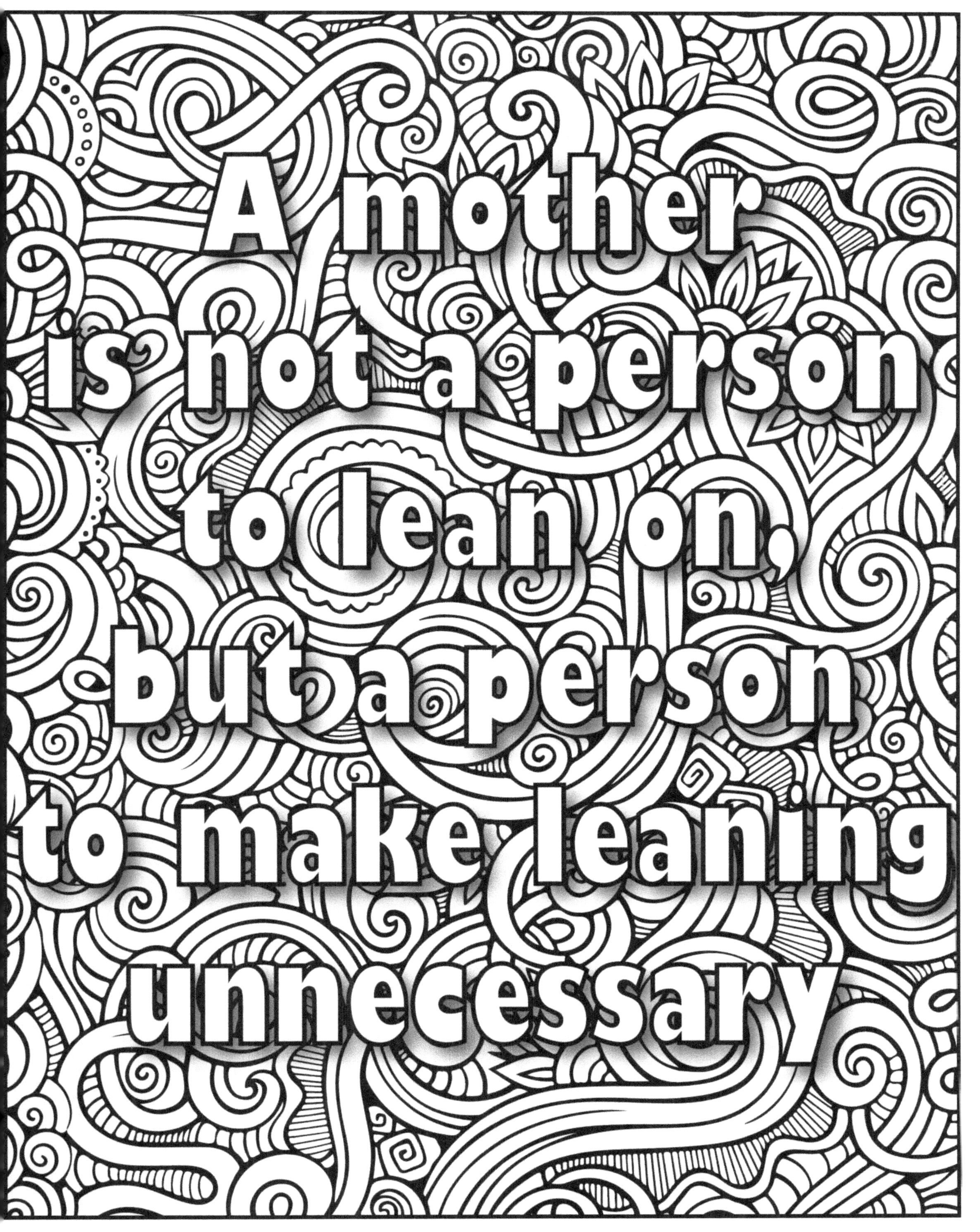
A mother
is not a person
to lean on,
but a person
to make leaning
unnecessary

If evolution really works, how come mothers only have two hands?

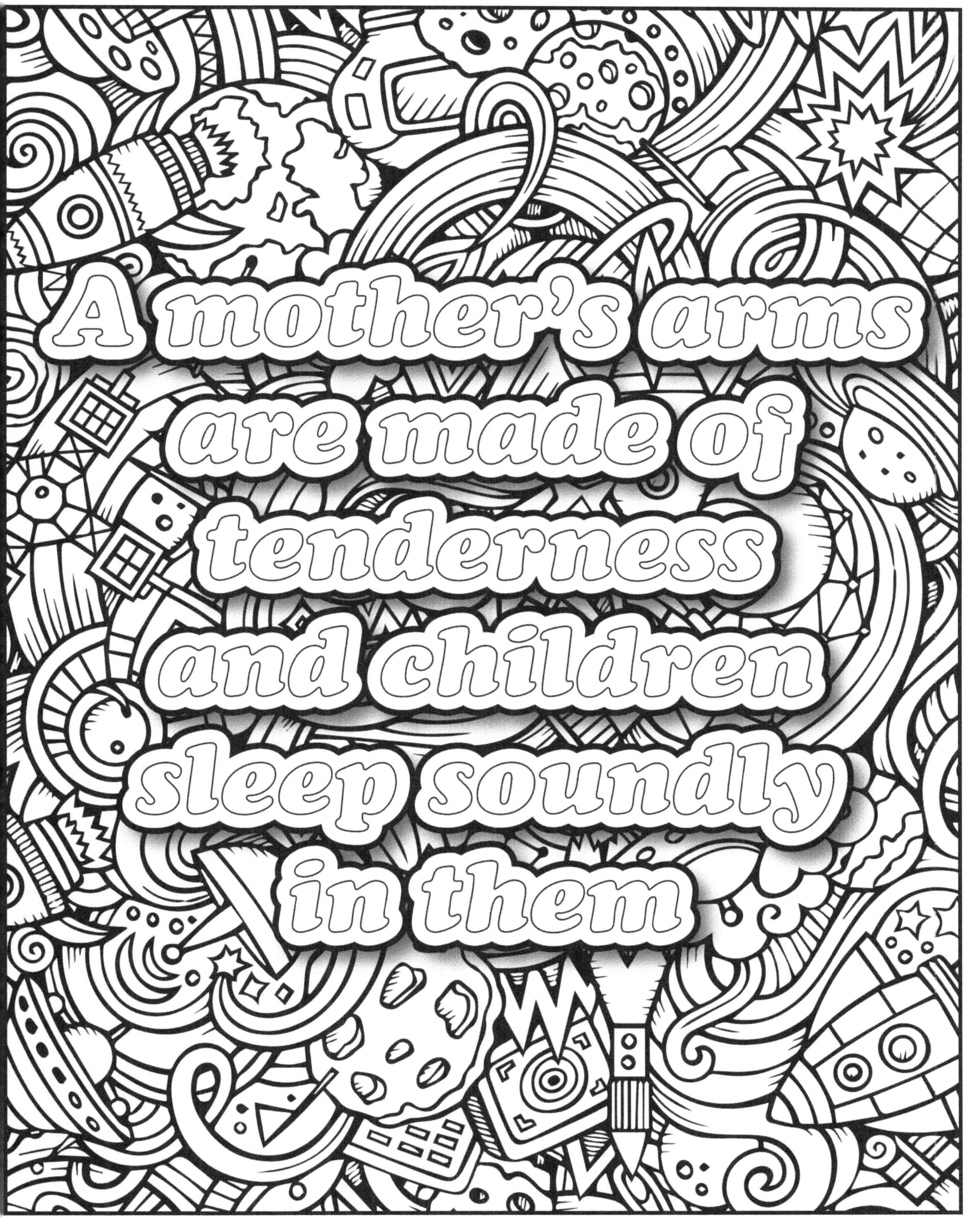

A mother's arms are made of tenderness and children sleep soundly in them

All mothers are working mothers

To the world,
you are
a mother.
But to
your family
you are
the world

I never knew
how much love
my heart could
hold until
someone called
me mommy

Most mothers
are instinctive
philosophers

Your children don't want a perfect mom, they want a happy mom

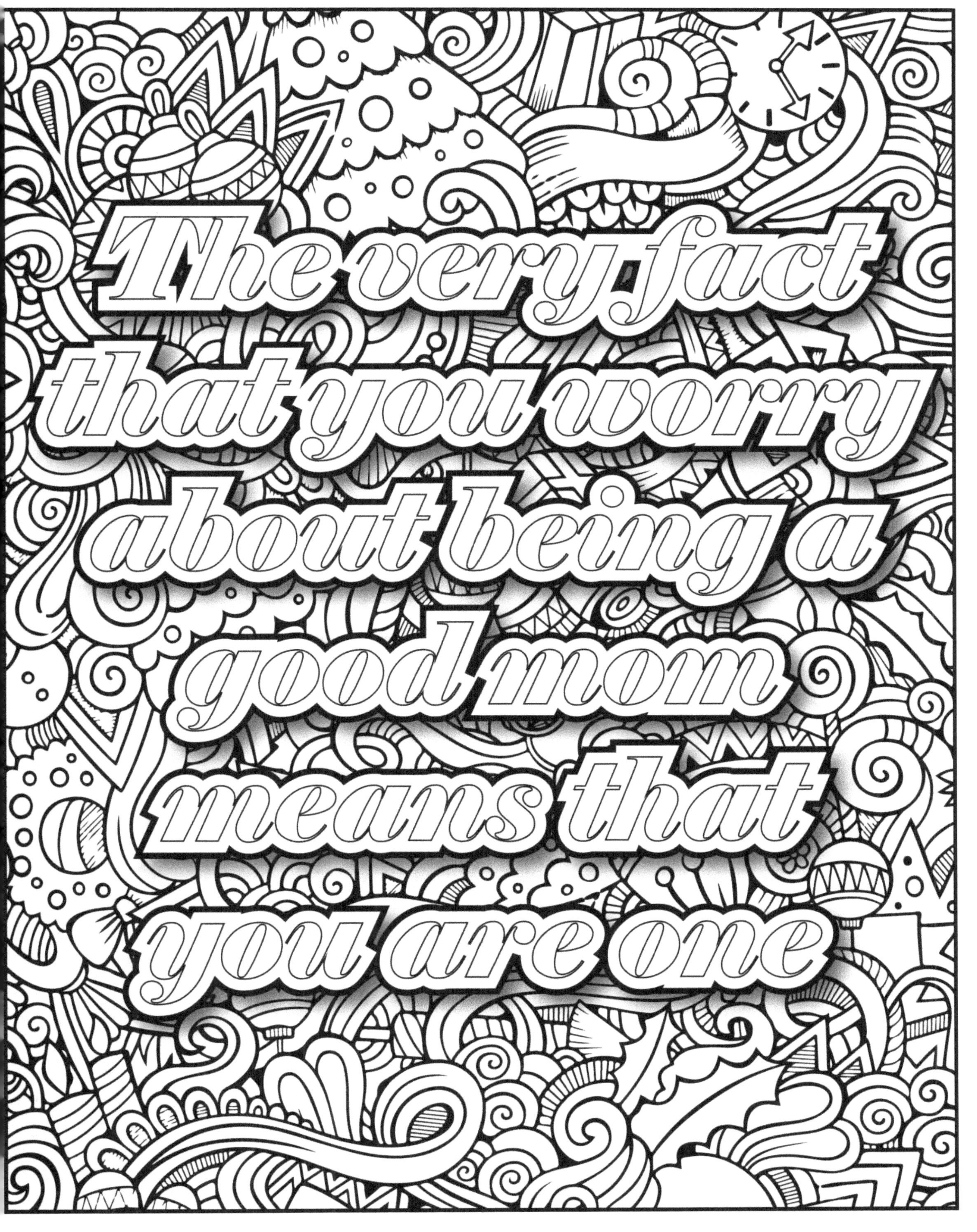

The very fact
that you worry
about being a
good mom
means that
you are one

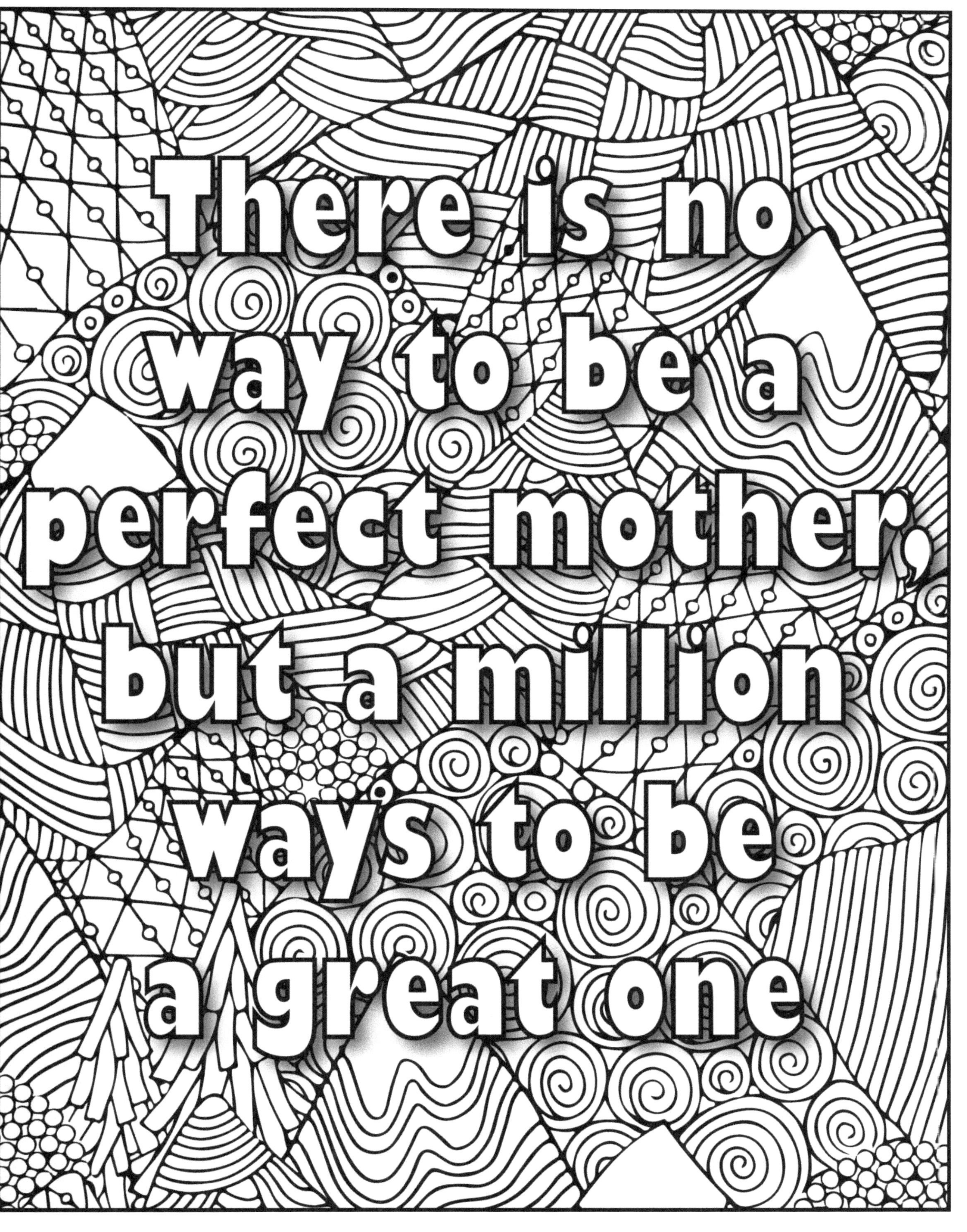

There is no way to be a perfect mother, but a million ways to be a great one

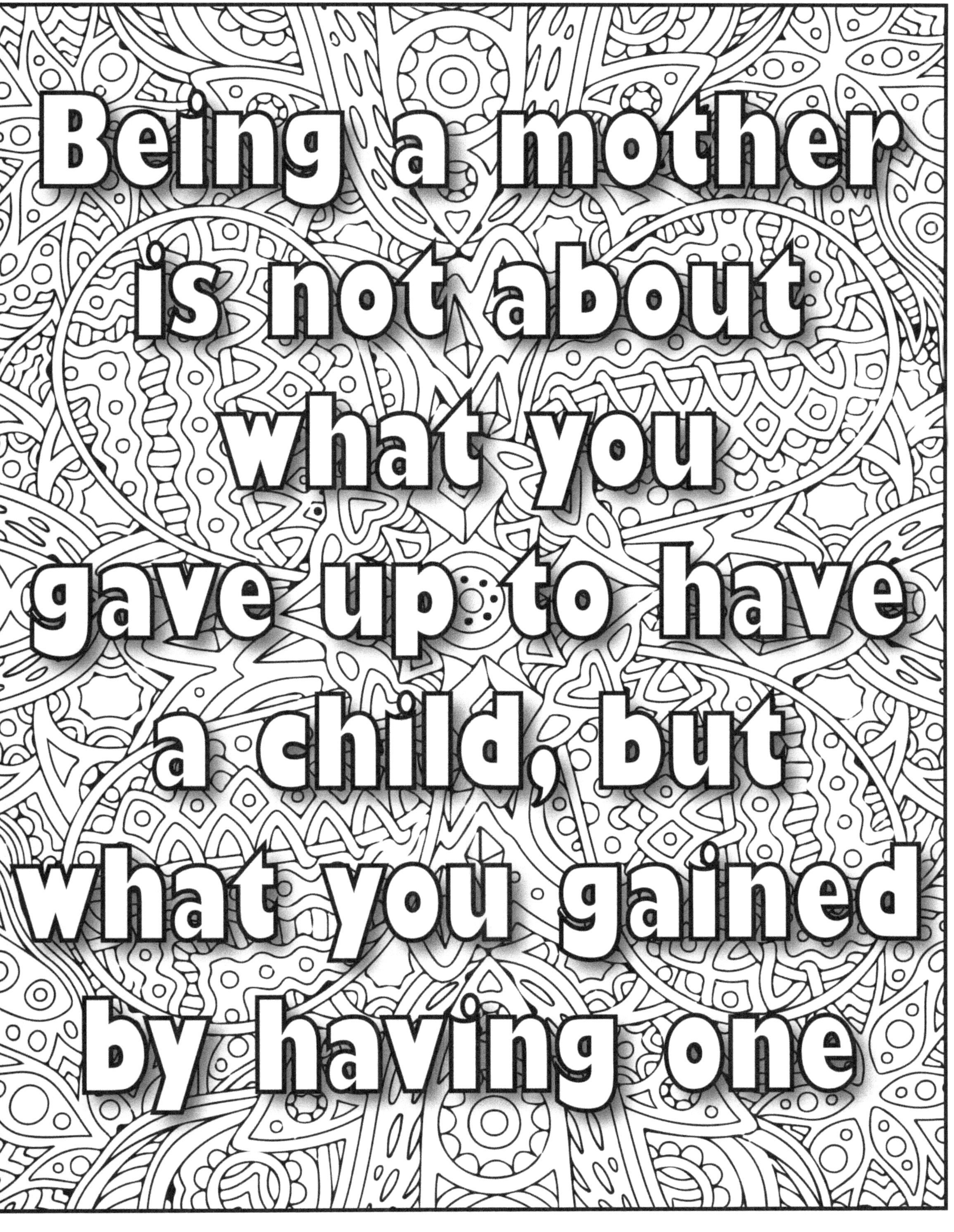
Being a mother
is not about
what you
gave up to have
a child, but
what you gained
by having one

Motherhood is
heart-exploding
blissful hysteria

It's the job that I take most seriously in my life and I think it's the hardest job

You Sacrificed for us. You're the real MVP

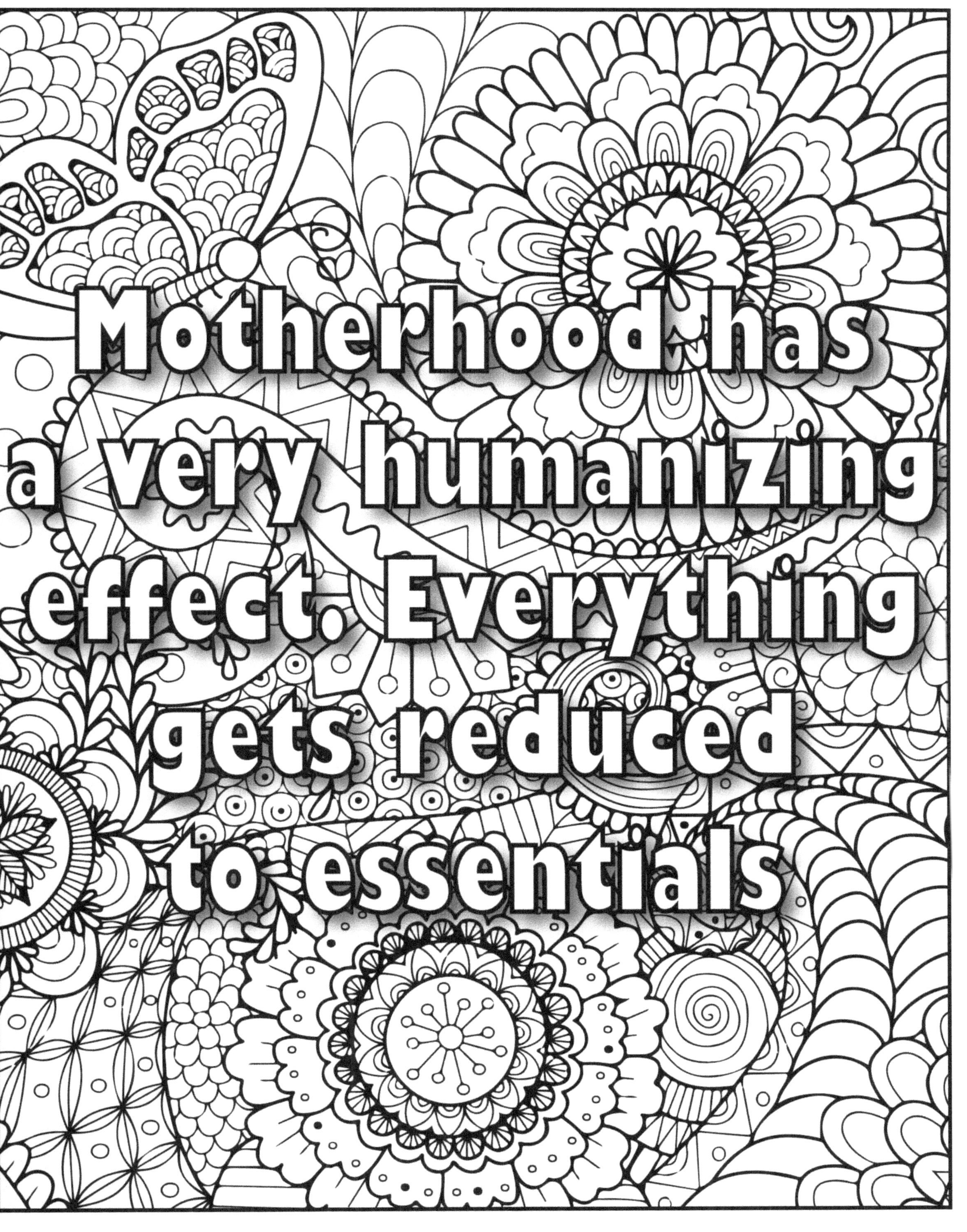

Motherhood has a very humanizing effect. Everything gets reduced to essentials

Motherhood is
the biggest
gamble
in the world

Whatever else is unsure in this stinking dunghill of a world a mother's love is not

A mother is
one to whom
you hurry
when you
are troubled

Everybody wants
to Save the Earth;
nobody wants
to help Mom
do the dishes

Successful mothers are not the ones that never struggled. They are the ones that never give up

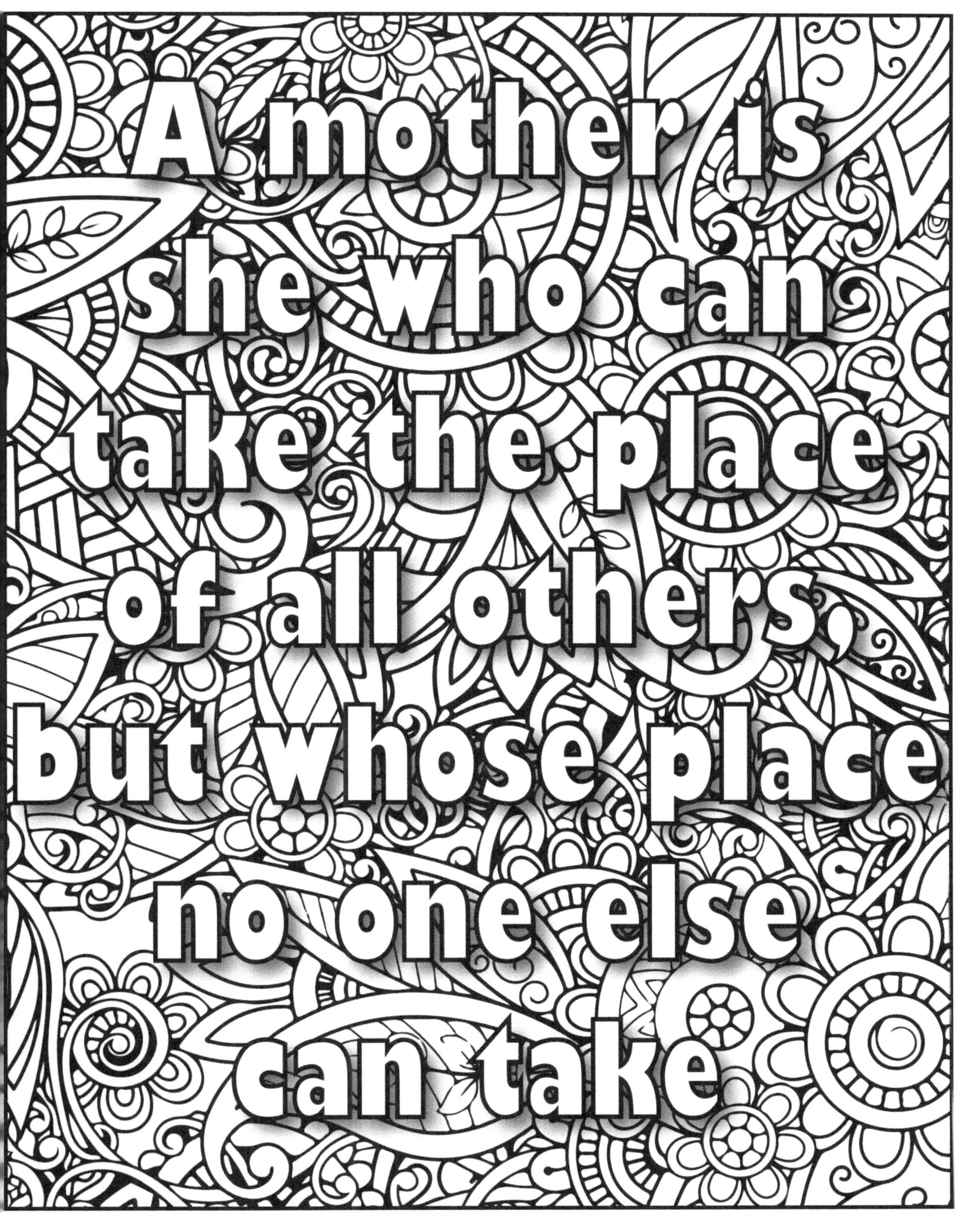

A mother is she who can take the place of all others, but whose place no one else can take

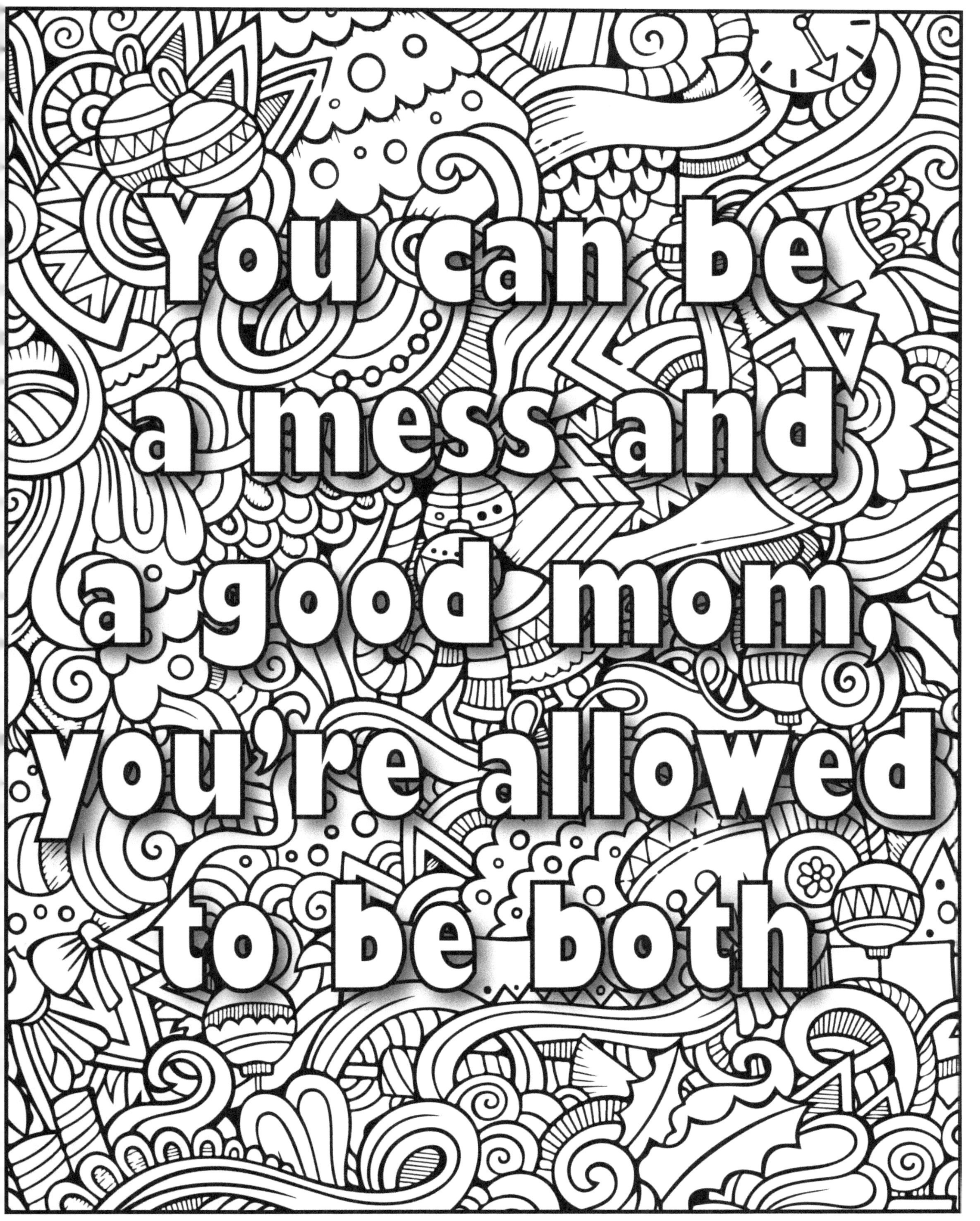
You can be
a mess and
a good mom,
you're allowed
to be both

We may not be perfect mothers, but we are perfect mothers for our children

Don't let
your struggle
become
your identity

Grow through what you go through

Don't count
the days
make them
count

It is
not stress
that kills us,
it is
our reaction
to it

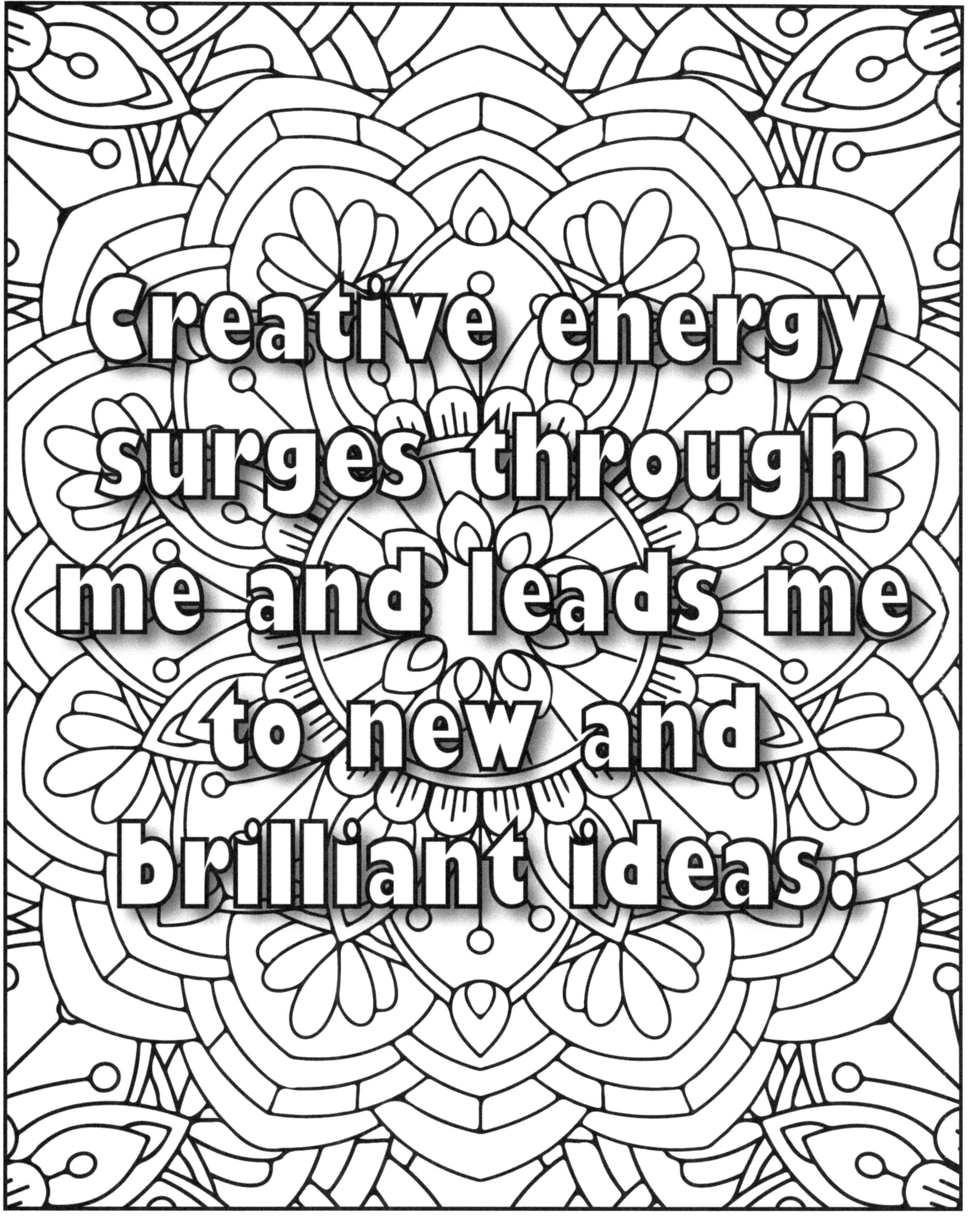

Creative energy surges through me and leads me to new and brilliant ideas.

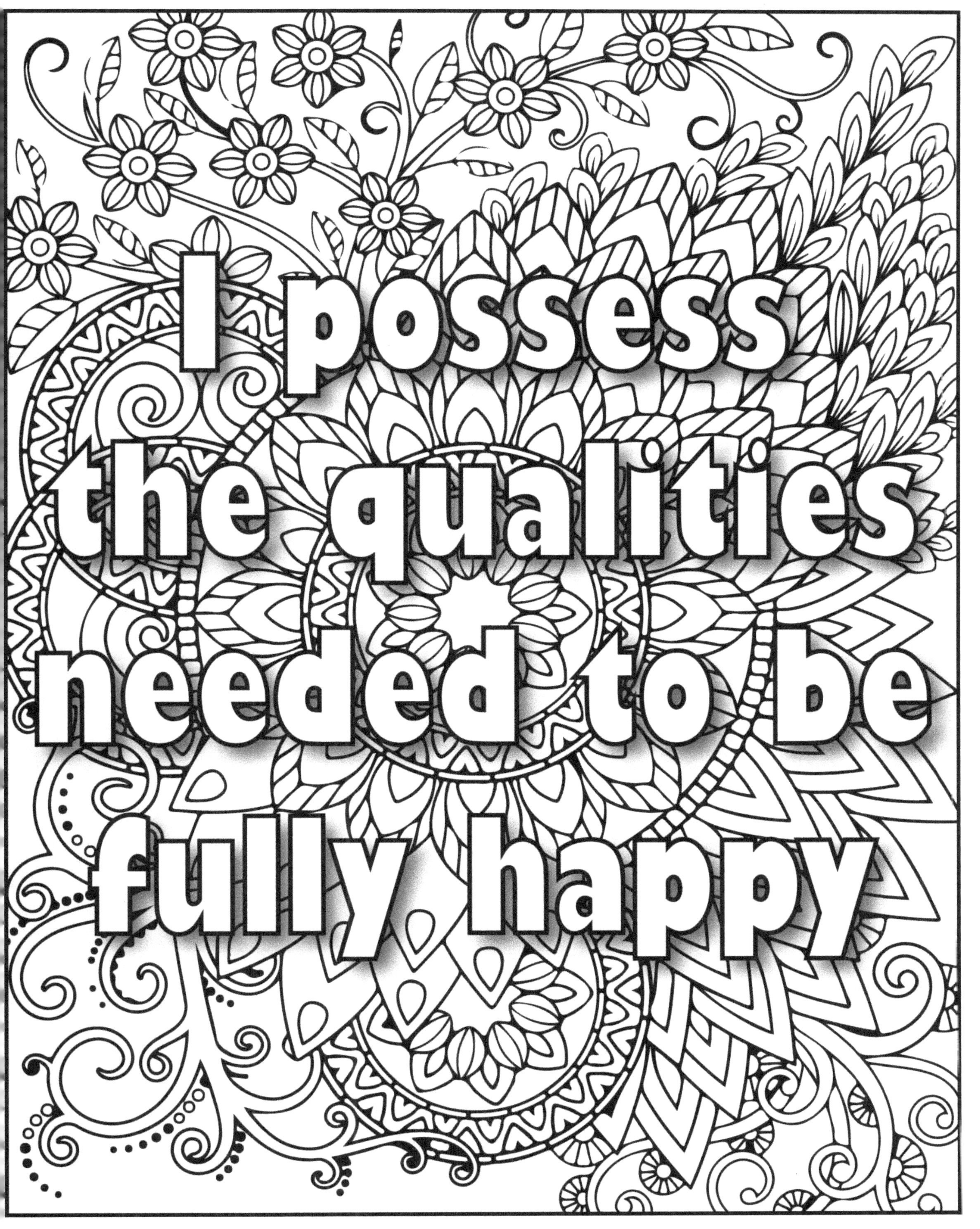

I possess
the qualities
needed to be
fully happy

Happiness
is
a choice

I wake up today with strength in my heart and clarity in my mind

I radiate beauty, charm, and grace

I am a powerhouse; I am indestructible

Today and
every day
I am enough

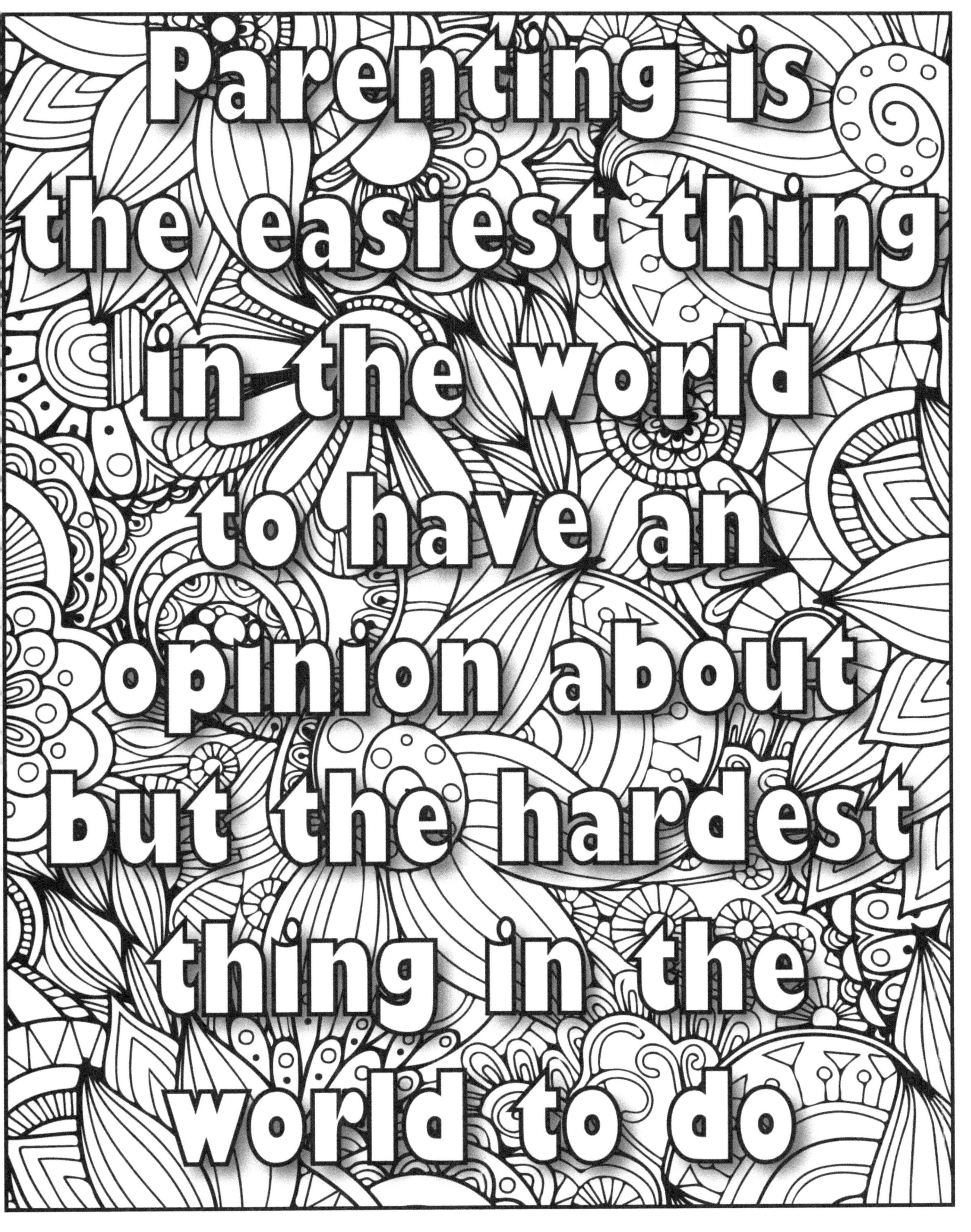

Parenting is the easiest thing in the world to have an opinion about but the hardest thing in the world to do

I am
courageous
and I stand up
for myself.

Today I am
enthusiastic
and full of
energy